PRAISE

We Are Made to Praise!

"Children of every race will see their faces in this beautiful book, as they are invited to praise the Lord along with sea creatures, stormy winds, and trees of the field. As a pastor, I am grateful to Esther Ruth Blair for this colorful and captivating resource for ministry with children."

—HENRY G. BRINTON, pastor of Fairfax Presbyterian Church in Virginia and author of the novel *City of Peace*

"*We Are Made to Praise!* is a vibrant, life-affirming book with a profound spiritual message. The beautiful artwork perfectly matches the inspirational text from Psalm 148."

—STEVE METZGER, award-winning author of *Detective Blue* and *Pluto Visits Earth!*

"*We Are Made to Praise!* is a beautiful, engaging presentation of God's Word that will invite children into His love from an early age."

—ALYSSA DEROSE, author of *Momoir: A New Mom's Journey to Embracing Her Not-So-Perfect Motherhood*

"This divinely illustrated and engaging book nourishes and sustains the natural spiritual attunement that babies come into this world with, all the while nurturing a grateful and tender relationship with God and all his creations."

—JULIANNE HAYCOX, author of *Conversations with Grace*

We Are Made to Praise!
by Esther Ruth Blair

ISBN 978-1-64663-466-8

Published by

An imprint of

3705 Shore Drive
Virginia Beach, VA 23455
800-435-4811
www.koehlerbooks.com

We Are Made to
Praise!

From Psalm 148

Written and Illustrated by
Esther Ruth Blair

For William,
our joy and little light.

PRAISE THE LORD!

Praise the Lord from the heavens

Praise Him,
all His heavenly hosts

Praise Him, sun

Praise Him, moon

Praise Him,
all you shining stars

Praise Him,
you highest heavens

Let the entire universe

praise the name

of the *Lord*

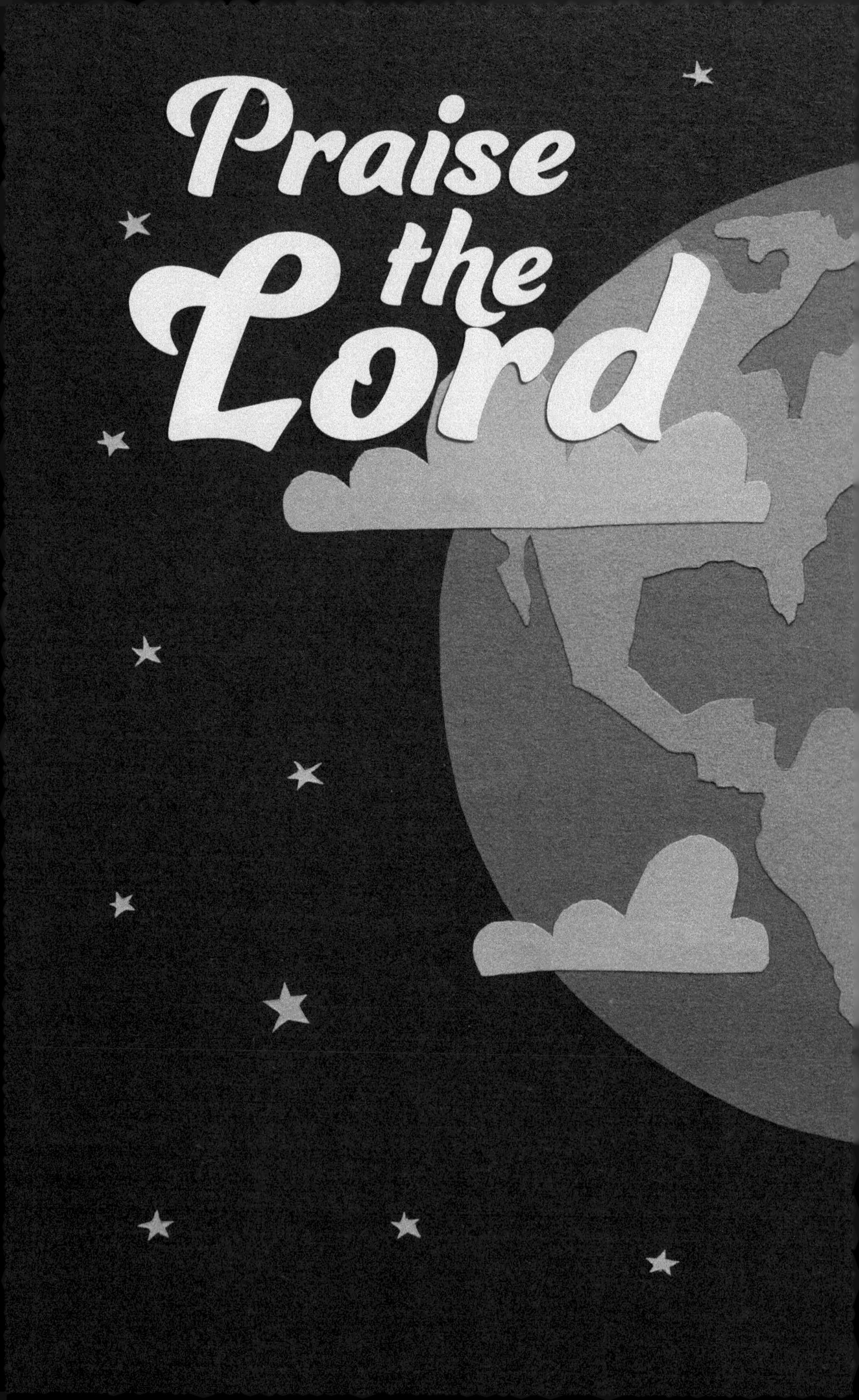
Praise
the
Lord

from the
Earth

Praise Him,
sea creatures

and all
ocean
depths

Praise Him, lightning

Praise Him, snow and clouds

Praise Him,
stormy winds

Praise Him, mountains and hills

Praise Him,
trees of the forest and field

Praise Him,
wild animals and small creatures

Praise Him, flying birds

Praise Him, kings and queens

old and
young alike

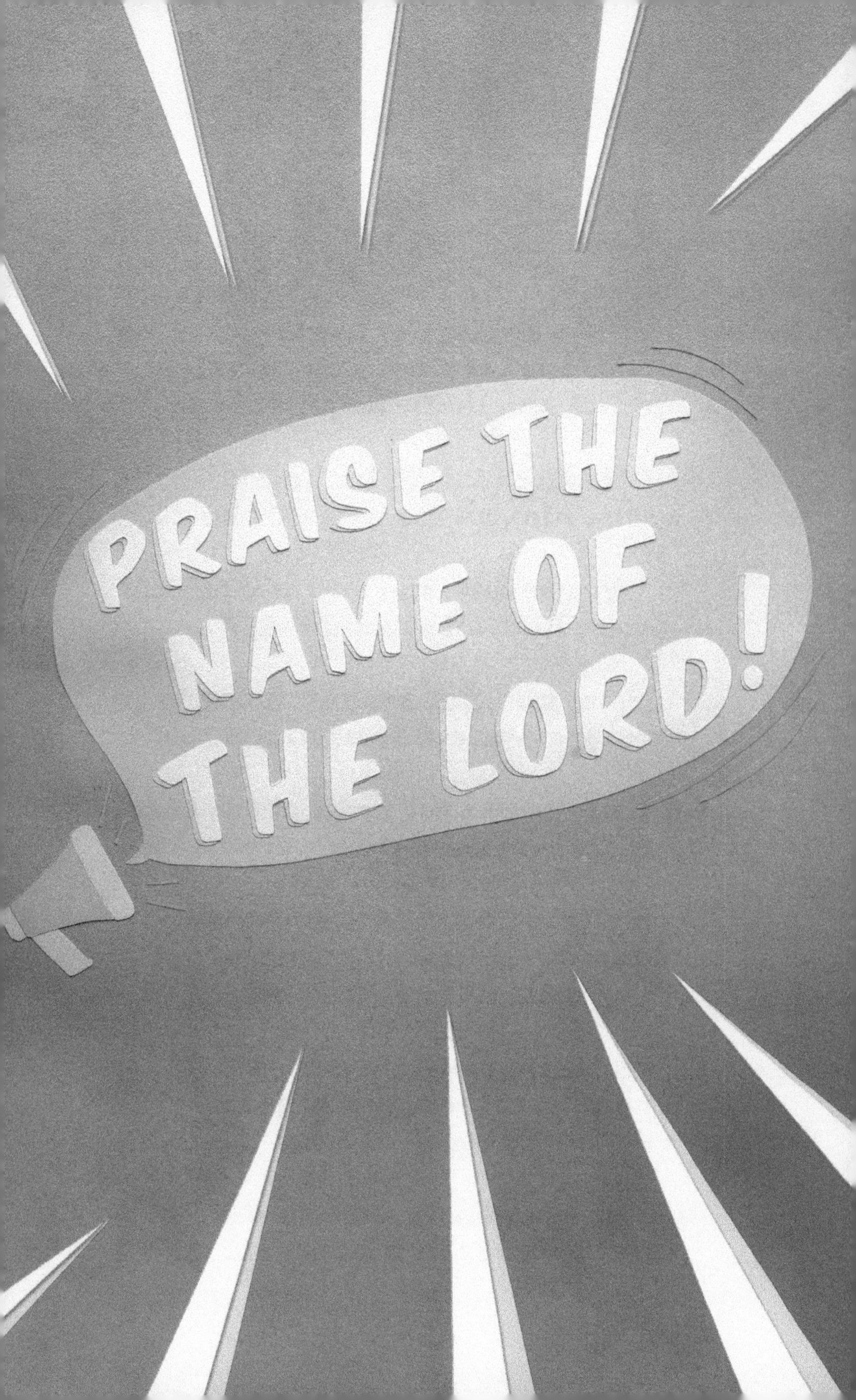
PRAISE THE NAME OF THE LORD!

Psalm 148, NIV

Praise the Lord.
Praise the Lord from the heavens;
praise him in the heights above.

Praise him, all his angels;
praise him, all his heavenly hosts.

Praise him, sun and moon;
praise him, all you shining stars.

Praise him, you highest heavens
and you waters above the skies.

Let them praise the name of the Lord,
for at his command they were created,

and he established them for ever
and ever—he issued a decree that
will never pass away.

Praise the Lord from the earth,
you great sea creatures and
all ocean depths,

lightning and hail, snow and clouds,
stormy winds that do his bidding,

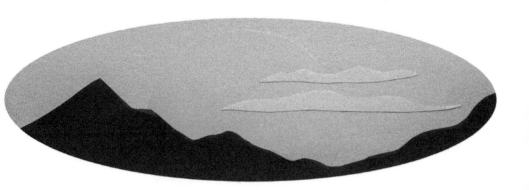

you mountains and all hills,
fruit trees and all cedars,

wild animals and all cattle,
small creatures and flying birds,

kings of the earth and all nations,
you princes and all rulers on earth,

young men and women,
old men and children.

Let them praise the name of the Lord,
for his name alone is exalted; his splendor
is above the earth and the heavens.

And he has raised up for his people a horn,
the praise of all his faithful servants,
of Israel, the people close to his heart.

Praise the Lord.

Acknowledgements

Thank you to my amazing husband, Robby Blair, for going above and beyond in helping this book become a reality. From encouraging me every step of the way to making sure I was able to set aside time to complete it to helping me put it together and choosing the best font to match the theme and design, you are the best partner. Will and I are so lucky to have you as ours.

Thank you to Laura Lowther at Progressive Printing for helping me with the very first copy I made for Will. Your expertise and confidence in me were inspiring and helped me through the process.

And thank you to Jenny DiCola for photographing all the pages and being patient with me when I had changes and needed to photograph again . . . and again.

CPSIA information can be obtained
at www.ICGtesting.com
Printed in the USA
BVHW090014060821
613738BV00014B/268